PICTURE A COUNTRY

China

Henry Pluckrose

W
FRANKLIN WATTS
A Division of Grolier Publishing
NEW YORK • LONDON • HONG KONG • SYDNEY
DANBURY, CONNECTICUT

This is the Chinese flag.

Photographic acknowledgements:
Cover: Holt Studios tr, Axiom br (above),
Robert Harding bl.

Insides: AKG London pp. 17b (Erich Lessing), Axiom
Photographic Agency pp. 11 (Gordon D.R. Clements), 21
(Gordon D.R. Clements), 25b (Gordon D.R. Clements)
Colorific! pp. 17t (Woodfin Camp/Kim Newton), 27l
(Contact/Dilip Mehta) Robert Harding pp. 8 (Jane
Sweeney),12 (Jane Sweeney), 25t (W. Guizman), 29 Holt
Studios pp. 18 (Inga Spence), 22 (Inga Spence) Impact
Photos pp. 10 (Christophe Bluntzer), 13 (Mark Henley), 12
(Mark Henley), 23t (Mark Henley), 23b (Mark Henley),
27r (Christophe Bluntzer) Magnum Photos pp. 19t (Michael
Nicholls), 26 (Rene Burri) Panos Pictures pp. 15 (R. Giling)
Planet Earth Pictures pp. 9 (Jan Tove Johansson), 19b
(Jan Tove Johansson), Popperfoto pp. 16 (Robyn Beck), 24
(Dave Joiner), Spectrum Colour Library p. 28 Still Pictures
p. 20 (Catherine Platt)

All other photography Steve Shott

Map by Julian Baker.
Series editor: Rachel Cooke
Series designer: Kirstie Billingham
Editor: Alex Young
Picture research: Sue Mennell

First published in 1999 by Franklin Watts
First American edition 1999 by
Franklin Watts
A division of Grolier Publishing
90 Sherman Turnpike
Danbury, CT 06816

Visit Franklin Watts on the Internet at:
http://publishing.grolier.com

Pluckrose, Henry Arthur.
     China / Henry Pluckrose.
        p. cm. -- (Picture a country)
     Includes index.
     Summary: A simple introduction to the geography,
people, culture and interesting sites of China.
     ISBN 0-531-14500-X (lib. bdg.) 0-531-15375-4 (pbk.)
     1. China--Juvenile literature. [1. China.] I. Title.
II. Series: Pluckrose, Henry Arthur. Picture a country.
DS706.P57 1999
951--dc21   98-36437
                                                         CIP
                                                          AC

Copyright © Franklin Watts 1999
Printed in Great Britain

GROLIER
PUBLISHING

Contents

Where Is China?

This is a map of China.
China is in Asia.
It is the third largest
country in the world.

China is divided into
different areas
called provinces.

Here are some
Chinese stamps
and money.
Chinese money is
counted in Yuan.

The Chinese Landscape

China is sometimes called "the land of mountains". It also has great rivers, deserts, and high, flat plains.

The steep sides of this valley in Guizhou province have been cut into terraces to make them easier to farm.

The Huang Shan (Yellow Mountains) in the Anhui province are famous for their strange shapes.

In the north of China, the summers are hot and the winters are cold and dry. In southern and central China, the weather is warm and humid throughout the year.

The Chinese People

People have lived in the country we call China for over 500 thousand years. China has the largest population in the world — over 1.2 billion people live there.

In some country villages, people have lived in the same way for thousands of years.

The Chinese people are part of an ancient civilization. Their way of writing is one of the oldest in the world.

Most of China's population lives in the south and east of the country.

Where They Live

Although most Chinese people live and work in the countryside, China has many large cities.

Most Chinese people live in small farming villages like this one in Guizhou province.

Nearly 14 million people live in the busy city of Shanghai.

Some of the largest Chinese cities are Hong Kong, Shanghai, Tianjin, and Wuhan.

The Capital City

Beijing is the capital of China. Beijing has been the most important city in China since the 14th century.

Today nearly 11 million people live in the modern city of Beijing.

This flag is flying in Tiananmen Square in Beijing.

At Work

Chinese factories make many things — from farm machinery and aircraft to bicycles and electrical goods. Mining is also important. Iron and tin are mined from the ground, as well as coal, oil, and natural gas.

More than 4 million bicycles are made in factories in Shanghai every year.

Many factories in China make electrical goods that are then sold in other countries.

Chinese factories make textiles such as silks and cottons. China produces half the world's silk. Chinese pottery, or china, has been sold all over the world for hundreds of years.

Farming

Two out of every three people in China work on the land. They grow crops of rice, wheat, sugar, soybeans, tea, fruit, vegetables, and cotton.

Traditional ways of farming and fishing are still very common in China.

This man is watering his rice crop.

Farmers also raise animals such as chickens, pigs, and cattle. They grow bamboo, which is used to make furniture.

These farmers are harvesting potatoes.

Home and School

Chinese families live close together. Grandparents, parents, and children often share the same house or apartment.

The Chinese language
does not have an alphabet.
Instead, each word has a
different shape.
Children have to learn in
school how to write each
different sign, or character.

Chinese Food

People in different parts of China enjoy different kinds of food. What food is eaten — and how it is cooked — depends on the region. At mealtimes people share dishes with their family and friends.

Chinese people buy vegetables fresh from the market. Green onions are used in many Chinese dishes.

Food is chopped into small pieces so that it will cook quickly.

People eat chicken, duck, lamb, fish, or pork, with vegetables and rice or noodles. Rice or noodles are eaten with nearly every meal.

Green tea is often drunk before a meal. Soup is eaten at the meal's end.

People eat with chopsticks instead of knives and forks.

Out and About

The Chinese enjoy many different sports, including soccer, track and field, swimming, and table tennis. Chinese table-tennis teams are very successful.

Linghui Kong plays for China in the table-tennis World Championships.

The yi trumpet is a popular Chinese instrument.

Chinese people also like listening to music and going to the opera.

Festivals and Religion

China has many festivals each year. Some celebrate the country's government; others celebrate religious beliefs.

On May Day there are huge parades all over the country.

Music and dance play an important part in many religious ceremonies.

Confucius, Lao Tzu, and Buddha were philosophers. Chinese people still follow their teachings today.

Visiting China

Tourists come to China to visit its temples and museums and to travel through its beautiful countryside.

The Great Wall of China was built over 2,000 years ago to protect China from invaders. It is 3,750 miles (6,030 km) long.

The Temple of Heaven in Beijing is where people go to pray for a good harvest.

Index

About This Book

The last decade of the 20th century has been marked by an explosion in communications technology. The effect of this revolution upon the young child should not be underestimated. The television set brings a cascade of ever-changing images from around the world into the home, but the information presented is only on the screen for a few moments before the program moves on to consider some other issue.

Instant pictures, instant information do not easily satisfy young children's emotional and intellectual needs. Young children take time to assimilate knowledge, to relate what they already know to ideas and information that are new.

The books in this series seek to provide snapshots of everyday life in countries in different parts of the world. The images have been selected to encourage the young reader to look, to question, to talk. Unlike the TV picture, each page can be studied for as long as is necessary and subsequently returned to as a point of reference. For example, the Chinese landscape might be compared with their own, or a discussion might develop about the ways in which food is prepared and eaten in a country whose culture and customs are different from their own.

The comparison of similarity and difference is the recurring theme in each of the titles in this series. People in different lands are superficially different. Where they live (the climate and terrain) obviously shapes the sort of houses that are built, but people across the world need shelter; coins may look different, but in each country people use money.

At a time when the world seems to be shrinking, it is important for children to be given the opportunity to focus upon those things that are common to all the peoples of the world. By exploring the themes touched upon in the book, children will begin to appreciate that there are strands in the everyday life of human beings that are universal.